MAP MAKING

ILLUSTRATED WITH MAPS AND DRAWINGS BY JUDITH HOFFMAN CORWIN AND PHOTOGRAPHS

JULIAN MESSNER NEW YORK

KARIN N. MANGO

All rights reserved including the right of
reproduction in whole or in part in any form.
Published by Julian Messner,
A Division of Simon & Schuster, Inc.
Simon & Schuster Building,
1230 Avenue of the Americas,
New York, New York 10020.
JULIAN MESSNER and colophon are trademarks of
Simon & Schuster, Inc.

Manufactured in the United States of America

Library of Congress Cataloging in Publication Data.

Mango, Karin N.
    Mapmaking.

    Bibliography: p.
    Includes index.
    Summary: Describes the techniques of making a map,
the meaning of various symbols used, how to read a map,
different kinds of maps and their purpose, and the
history of mapmaking.
    1. Maps—Juvenile literature. [1. Maps] I. Corwin,
Judith Hoffman, ill. II. Title.
GA130.M37 1984   912   83-25084
ISBN 0-671-45518-4

Picture Credits

The Long Island Historical Society, p. **23**
NASA, pp. **74, 88, 90**
Marie Tharp, pp. **81, 83, 84**
United Nations, p. **38**
U.S. Geological Survey, pp. **10, 26**

To my father and the memory of my mother

ACKNOWLEDGMENTS

For permission to reproduce photographs, I am indebted to the National Maritime Museum, Greenwich, London; the dean and chapter of Hereford Cathedral, Hereford, England; the Long Island Historical Society, Brooklyn, New York; the U.S. Geological Survey; the National Aeronautics and Space Administration (NASA); and the United Nations, New York.

Thanks are also due to Marie Tharp, oceanographic cartographer, for permission to reproduce the diagram and photograph on pages 83 and 84; and to Oliver J. Corwin for permission to use his map, on page 98.

And to my family, gratitude for their perceptive comments and continuing moral support.

CONTENTS

1 WORLD AROUND YOU

Where do you live? You might answer:

39 East Walnut Street
Summertown, Massachusetts
U.S.A.

And you might add:

The World
The Universe
Outer Space

That is a fairly clear address. However, what does it really say about where you live? What it is like?

You know that Summertown is medium-sized and the Lincoln River runs through the middle of it. You know that the country is hilly, with small lakes. You're proud that Summertown is known for its college and its boot factory.

How would you find this town if you were a stranger? How would you tell someone directions to get to Summertown?

You would probably say, "Look at a map."

The following is a map of the United States:

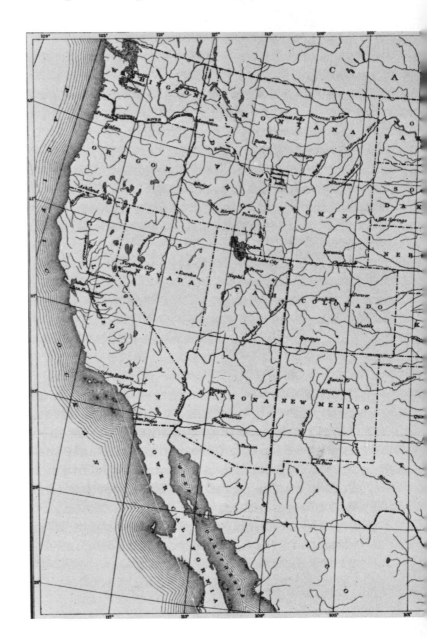

3

Summertown seems to have vanished. There is just too much on that map and everything is far too small. How about this?

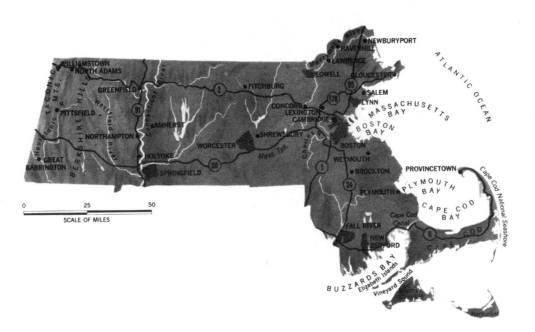

This map may not show Summertown, but you get the picture, and there's certainly plenty in it. Yet not all the information you want is there. And there's a lot you don't understand on the map and in the sets of numbers and letters around the edge. You may feel a bit confused.

That is because there are maps—and then there

4

are maps, and each kind tells a different story. Let's begin again. Where do you live?

Home.

You know where you are in home territory. You know your way around. To go to school you turn right outside your house, go down East Walnut to the circle, continue straight on to the old church, and so on.

You know. But what happens if you invite Nick, a friend who is new in the neighborhood and has never been to your house before? You've already been to his house, so you know the way there. How do you guide him back? You could give him a list of streets to follow. But it would be much clearer for him to have a picture to look at showing all he needs to know: a **map**.

You don't have to create a masterpiece out of an atlas. In fact, your sketch map will be better because you know what your friend should look for on his way to your house.

The biggest problem in drawing a map is determining size. How do you get a big chunk of town onto a small piece of paper? You do it by scaling it down, drawing it in miniature. You represent a street half a mile long by drawing a short line. You draw the big buildings that make up your school as a small square. Instead of the wide, curving Lincoln River, you draw a thin, curving line. A couple of trees represent the whole park.

Just making things small isn't enough. You have to draw them in proportion to each other. One block must look the same length as the next on the map if they are the same length in real life. Nick must have an idea of how far he has to go and be able to trust your map. And though he doesn't need to know where the North and South Poles are, he needs to know the general direction he's going in—north, south, east, or west—so he doesn't get lost.

When you draw a map, you have to decide which way is up: the reader has to look at it from a fixed point. Since maps are usually drawn with north at the top, you will want to use the top of your paper for north.

Where is north? The sun rises in the east and sets in the west. At midday, the sun is at its most southerly point. The opposite end is north. How does your street lie with regard to north and south? Go outside and check.

Landmarks will also help keep Nick on course: the school, the gas station, the church. Be selective and leave out what's not important. He doesn't have to know about the hospital four blocks beyond your house. Crowding the map will confuse, not help him. Clean lines and clear directions are what you're aiming at.

Now let's start drawing. You will need a good-sized piece of paper. Maybe more than one, if your first try doesn't work out so well. You will also need a pencil with a good point, a sharpener, some colors, an eraser, and a ruler.

You have decided on indicating north and how your street and house line up with north, and the general direction between your house and Nick's.

Mark north at the top. Put your house near the edge of the paper so that you can use the whole sheet to show the streets along Nick's route.

The beginning of your sketch map might look something like this:

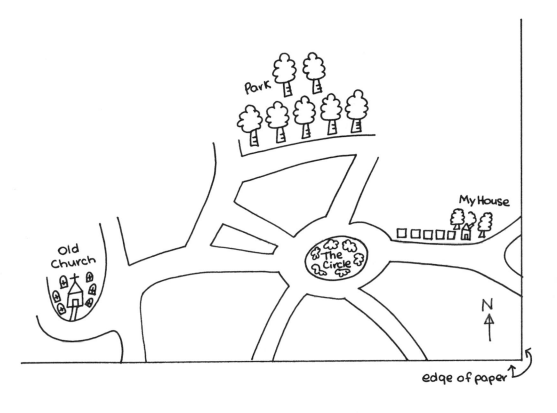

Put in the landmarks as little drawings or symbols. You could show the church as a square with a cross on top. As long as the symbols are clear, you don't have to explain them. Those that need it can be explained off to the side of your map in what is known as a **key** or **legend**.

This is what the completed sketch map for Nick might look like:

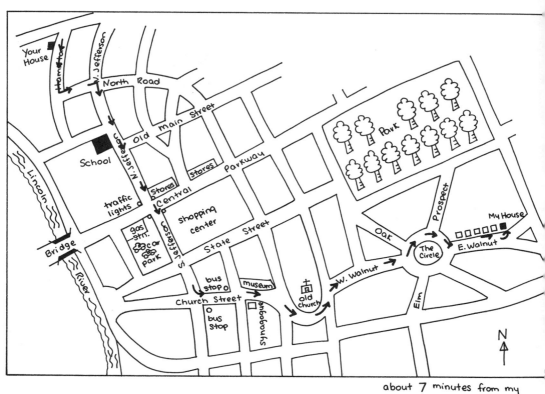

about 7 minutes from my house to the old church

When Nick arrives, you'll know right away how well the map worked—if he hadn't already called you to say he was lost. Did he arrive smiling or frowning? Maybe everything worked out perfectly. You hope so. But maybe he had a little trouble at that crossing by the shopping center. Or you didn't show Church Street as long as it really is, and it seemed endless to him.

You might want to walk home with Nick to see where you were off, to correct the map. And you might want to check your map against a printed map of your town. Were you pretty close?

2 WORLD AT YOUR FEET

You can't always be in familiar territory. You don't even want to be.

Imagine that you're on vacation and a group of you wants to go on a hike. Helen has a map, but it doesn't look anything like the sketch map of your neighborhood that you drew for Nick. It isn't like the town map you looked at, either, full of streets and buildings. Helen's map looks something like this:

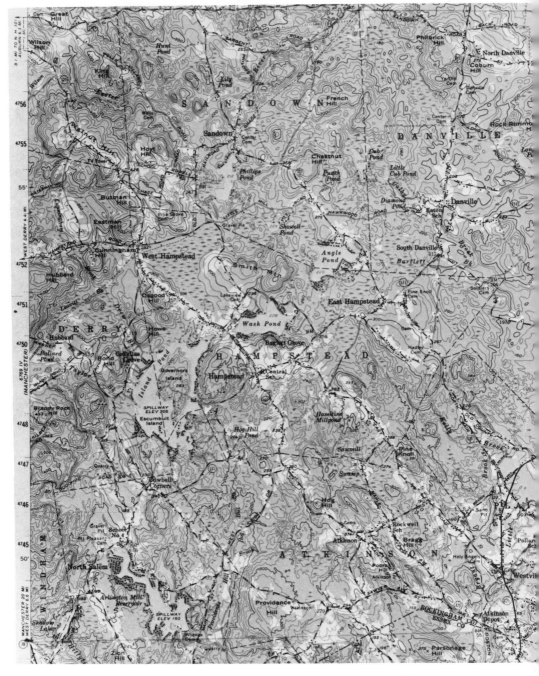

Topographical map of part of southern New Hampshire

The map is almost in another language. But map language is one you can easily learn. Look at Helen's map more closely. She ordered it from the U.S. Geological Survey in Arlington, Virginia. They make maps of various kinds for the whole country. This is a **topographical** map. A topographical map gives a geat deal of information in a small space: direction, distance, landmarks. It has everything you had on your sketch map, but it is accurately calculated and drawn to scale, using, for instance, one inch to represent one mile.

Drawing to scale is making an exact, miniaturized copy of the real thing. Helen's map is on a scale of 1:62,500. This means that one inch on the map is 62,500 inches on actual ground. That seems ridiculous until you realize that 62,500 inches almost exactly equals one mile. So one inch on the map is one mile on the ground.

A map is a picture of the landscape. This map is of countryside, so most of it is colored naturally in green and brown, with blue for water.

In order to show the terrain—flat, hilly, mountainous—topographical maps use **contours**. Look at the concentric lines (those having the same center) of Howe Hill. Each line shows the height of the land at a particular distance above sea level. The contour intervals are twenty feet, which means each line represents twenty more feet of height. If the contour lines are widely spaced, the slope is gentle. The closer the contour lines, the steeper the slope. Howe Hill is fairly steep.

Landmarks and special types of terrain are

shown by symbols, which are explained in the legend to the map. (Check page 46 for a list of the topographical symbols shown on this map—marsh, buildings, cemetery, boundary lines, different kinds of roads.)

How far do you want to go? Distances are deceptive on a map as everything looks so close. You need to know the scale of the map to plan how far you're going.

Imagine that you want to hike five miles. You want to start and end in Hampstead. That doesn't mean hiking five miles out because it would also mean five miles back. You want to hike two and a half miles out and the same back, or a five-mile circular trip. You decide to hike down Hampstead Main Street, along Island Pond shore to a picnic on Governor's Island, and back. But Governor's Island is wooded, the road is merely a track. It would be quite easy to lose your way there. You need to take a **compass** along to Governor's Island.

What is a compass for? Basically it's a security blanket. With a compass and common sense, you need never be totally lost. You can always get your bearings. If you have a compass but no map, you won't lose your direction. The compass will keep you facing the right way even if you can't see your objective, which may be behind a hill or beyond the horizon. If you feel you are lost, a compass gets you back on course.

If you use a compass and map together, you can know exactly where you are. You can identify landmarks, and get from here to there using the best route. You can use a map without a compass, but only if there are enough landmarks on the map to identify your whereabouts, and the weather is good enough to see them.

You can buy an inexpensive compass at a scout shop or any camping store. If possible, get a Silva compass on a plastic base with measurement markings like this:

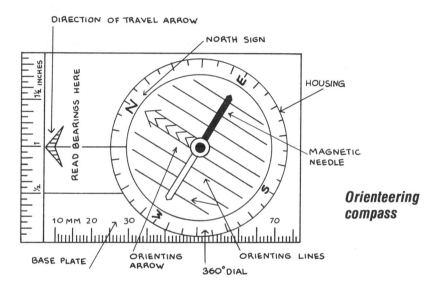

DIRECTION OF TRAVEL ARROW

NORTH SIGN

1¼ INCHES

READ BEARINGS HERE

HOUSING

MAGNETIC NEEDLE

Orienteering compass

10 MM 20   30   70

BASE PLATE

ORIENTING ARROW

ORIENTING LINES

360° DIAL

This is called an **orienteering compass**. Become familiar with it. North, south, east, and west are marked on the movable housing, covering the full 360° circle of directions in which you can go from any point.

There are three arrows on a Silva compass. Look at the striped arrow drawn in a fixed position facing north. But north seems to be facing any direction you want to point the striped arrow. You need to look at the wobbling, solid-color arrow or needle—red or black on your compass. That's the magnetized, north-seeking one. To get a bearing on north, line up the striped arrow and the third arrow, the one pointing in the direction of travel. Turn the whole compass around until the solid arrow is on top of the striped arrow. It's facing north. Actually it's facing **magnetic north**. Magnetic north shifts; true north does not.

Maps are based on true north, and the compass shows magnetic north. When using a compass and map together, you have to make an allowance for the difference between true and magnetic north: a diagram in the map margin shows the **decli-**

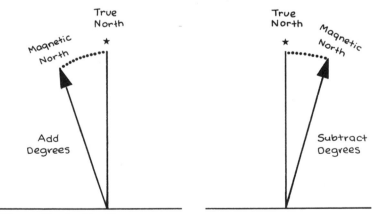

Magnetic declination

nation—"turning away" or difference—between true and magnetic north. To get true north, if the magnetic arrow in the margin diagram is to the right of true north, subtract the amount stated in the margin; if the arrow is to the left, add the amount.

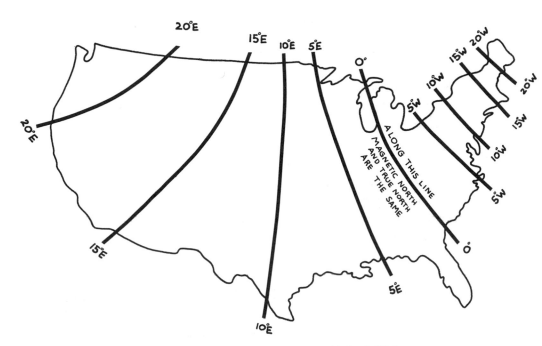

Degrees of magnetic declination across the United States

Even when using a map and compass for going short distances, the variation has to be taken into account. There is a difference of about 30 yards per mile for every degree of declination. If the declination in your area is 15°, 30 × 15 = 450 yards or a quarter mile. You could get truly lost if you do not calculate declination.

You don't need to know magnetic declination in two cases. The first is if you are using a compass without a map, because then you are using **field** or visual bearings and checking north with the sun. The other case is if you happen to be along the line where true and magnetic north coincide. The line runs through Ontario, Lake Superior, Wisconsin, Illinois, Kentucky, Tennessee, Alabama, and western Florida and is called the **Agonic Line**.

Now that you know the compass's peculiarities, you can practice getting your bearings at home. Where are you with respect to north? Line yourself up with north. Now, say you want to go east. The whole circle of possible directions, starting and ending at north, is 360°. East is a quarter of the way or 90° around the circle. Turn the movable compass housing until you line 90° up with the direction-of-travel arrow. Hold the compass horizontally in front of you, with the direction-of-travel arrow pointing ahead. Keep the compass away from any metal that might attract the magnetic needle. Still holding the compass the same way, turn yourself around till the magnetic needle is directly over the striped arrow and facing north. Now look where the direction-of-travel arrow is facing. That's east. Or you can say you are on a bearing of 90° east. Try getting your bearings for 180°, 45°, or any degree reading up to 360°.

Determine the direction and degree reading for

something you can see: maybe a big tree at the end of your street. With the compass horizontal, point the direction-of-travel arrow at the tree. Turn the compass housing until the magnetic needle is over the striped arrow facing north. The degree reading is now lined up with the direction-of-travel arrow.

Practice taking degree readings for other landmarks. Go from landmark to landmark. When you've reached the tree, take a bearing on the lamppost at the end of the next block. If that's too

Taking bearings

far, use a closer landmark first, one in line with the distant lamppost. This is what you would do on an actual hike when you can't see all the way to your goal. If you are not sure you are heading exactly the right way, check yourself by **backsighting**: without altering the compass, turn around to face your original landmark. The plain or south end of the magnetized needle should be over the fixed,

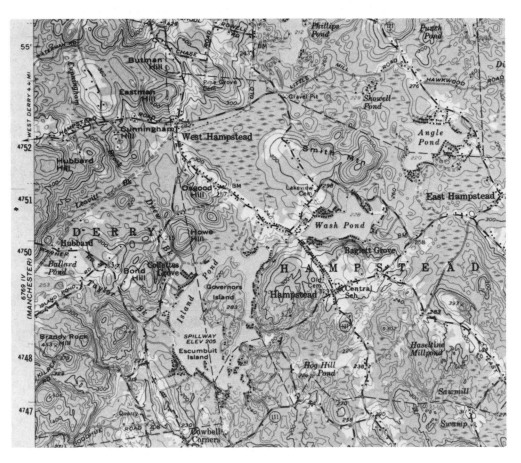

striped arrow. If it isn't, move around slowly until it is.

Now let's look at the map again. Which direction is it from Hampstead to Governor's Island? Put the edge of the compass base on the map along your route between Hampstead and Governor's Island, with the direction-of-travel arrow toward Governor's Island. Turn the housing of the compass till the fixed, striped arrow is parallel with the vertical—north-facing—edge of the map. Turn the map—with the compass on it—until the magnetic needle and the striped, orienting arrow are over each other at north. The degree reading for Governor's Island lines up with the direction-of-travel arrow. It's about due west, 260°. Take into account magnetic north and add the number in the map margin, 15½°. The direction is 275½°.

How far is it? Using the inch ruler on the compass base, see how many inches it is from the middle of Main Street to the edge of the island. Count off the measurement on the scale in the margin. It looks like just one inch, but remember that it is straight "as the crow flies," and walking along paths and up hills will be longer.

To gauge the distance accurately, you can use a handy pocket gadget called a **map measurer**. It has a wheel that you run on your map along the length of your route. The wheel registers the exact mileage of the trip on a dial, according to the scale of your particular map.

There are a couple of things to remember before you start your hike. Show the adults in charge of you exactly where you are going. It's a good idea to write it down for them. Tell them about how long you will be. It's common sense as well as common courtesy.

You will need the right clothes for the day: comfortable shoes or sneakers, a windbreaker or sweater, food and drink (not too much—you'll have to carry everything). And don't forget your topographical map and compass.

The first part along the sidewalk on Main Street is easy, and Helen leaves the map in her pocket. Now you reach your first turn. What is your bearing at the little patch of water near Wash Pond for Governor's Island? The formula indicates that $230 + 15\frac{1}{2} = 245\frac{1}{2}°$. It's hilly and wooded along the shore. The lake disappears from view. The road becomes an "unimproved dirt road" according to the legend. Actually it's an uneven track. Check the compass: pick out a couple of landmarks to get bearings. Still correct? The track is coming to an end. Now you're going southeast along the inlet. Your group takes the "light duty road" and heads northwest for the island. You can see the bridge to the island.

On the island, the "road" continues, very overgrown and wooded, but there's a pleasant picnic spot ahead. You are hot, hungry, and thirsty. You all hurry toward it.

After a while, full and rested, everyone decides to go further into the island before turning back. All of you wander into the cool, pleasant woods, staying together as a group so no one gets lost. But you haven't noticed how the path has disappeared in the undergrowth. Trees obscure the view. You don't recognize the landscape on the map. You forgot to stay aware of your surroundings, to check landmarks as you wandered. You're lost. But don't panic. First of all, stop, and keep your group together. You also have your compass. The bridge is about 135° east along the direction-of-travel arrow. You don't have to take magnetic declination into account since you are just using compass bearings at the moment. You may have to go off the true direction occasionally to go around overgrown areas, but your compass keeps you straight. You move on, picking out landmarks to aim for.

And suddenly, there's the path, and beyond it the bridge. In a short time, you'll be back in Hampstead telling everyone how you found your way with map and compass.

3 CHANGING WORLD

The maps of your town or Hampstead, New Hampshire, look as if they've always been that way. But if you think about it, you'll realize that nothing is permanently fixed on the map. In fact, the world is constantly changing. The shape of the land is altered by nature and by people. Sometimes the process is slow, like the natural erosion of coastal dunes by the seas. Changes can also be sudden. An erupting volcano like Mount St. Helens, or an avalanche, can alter a whole landscape. The moment a manmade dam starts to work, it changes the way everything looks for miles around.

One of the best ways to understand the gradual changes taking place over a long period of time, and how those changes show up on the map, is to follow the development of a city. Let's look at a particular place: Brooklyn, New York.

If it were independent of New York City, Brooklyn would be the fourth-largest city in the United States. Busy, built up, crowded and energetic, it spreads over the flat landscape of western Long Island, just across the water from Manhattan. Who would believe it was once hill and swamp, plains and forest, and full of deer, wolf, otter, and bear?

Indians were the earliest settlers in Brooklyn. They had plantations of corn and fished the surrounding waters. They lived off the land and were part of it.

The Dutch settled Brooklyn in the seventeenth century. They called it "Breukelen" after a town in Holland. They were farmers and divided the flat, open land along the shore into tracts for their cattle, orchards, houses, and mills. The face of the land was beginning to alter. The settlers did not make detailed maps themselves, but this is what the landscape looked like:

Dutch Brooklyn in the seventeenth century

The British ruled after the Dutch. And it was the colonists' rebellion against the British that put Brooklyn on the map. The important Revolutionary War battle of Long Island of August 1776 took place largely around Brooklyn. The British won, and Long Island—including Brooklyn—remained British until the end of the war. The British troops needed accurate maps, and careful surveys were made of Long Island's coast and interior.

The area was changing rapidly and growing fast. The original Dutch villages grew and flourished, covering more and more territory. New streets were laid out in the villages, with better roads to join them. The hills were low and sandy enough to be leveled easily. Breukelen—now known as Brookland or Brooklyn—grew fastest. It was well positioned, facing Manhattan, near the

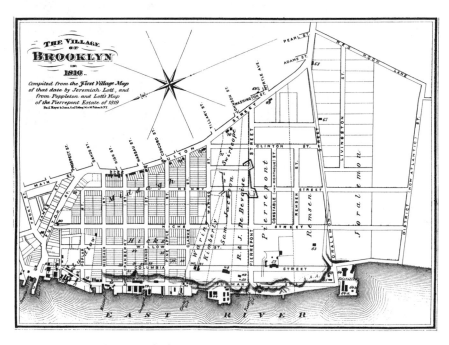

Brooklyn village, 1816

water for travel and shipping, and with farm country around to supply food. Brooklyn Heights, the area just over the river from Manhattan, was a popular spot where people built mansions as year-round or summer residences.

Soon the farms and market gardens in Brooklyn were broken up into lots for developers to build homes. The Gowanus Creek at the western end was deepened, ponds filled up, and marshland drained to make room for more houses, as more and more people moved across the river to Brooklyn. As it grew, Brooklyn absorbed neighboring settlements.

The structure of the landscape was altered, too. Running water was piped into houses. The Gowanus Creek was dredged and extended into a canal to make the harbor larger and safer. The Atlantic Docks changed the waterfront on one side and the government Navy Yard changed it on the other.

Fires change maps, too, and fires occurred frequently. The Great Fire of Brooklyn in the mid-nineteenth century devastated a thickly settled area, destroying many of the old buildings. Rebuilding changed architectural styles, widened the streets, and changed the map.

Better communication between Brooklyn and Manhattan became essential: the steam ferries were too limited. In 1883, the Brooklyn Bridge joined Brooklyn to New York once and for all, and sparked another building boom as property values soared. Homes pushed the remaining farms out. Commerce and industry flourished.

In 1898, Brooklyn formally became one of the five boroughs of New York City. The railroad began to cross Brooklyn on its way through Long Island. Subway tunnels were dug underneath. Other bridges were built—the latest, the soaring Verrazano-Narrows Bridge to Staten Island, in 1964. Highways expanded. More and more people came to live in Brooklyn.

Recreation areas were developed: Coney Island and other beaches at the edges, Prospect Park in the middle.

Brooklyn today is a major residential and commercial region, a center of domestic and foreign trade, with an extensive waterfront. However, the map constantly changes as a national park is developed in one area, landfill builds up another area for housing. . . .

Brooklyn today, aerial photograph

How about your own city or town? How did it begin? Why was it built where it is? What were the geographical reasons? How did history affect it? What was it like one hundred years ago? Fifty? Ten? Was it planned in a linear, rectangular, or radiating design like Washington, D.C.; Levittown, Pennsylvania; or Shaker Heights, Ohio?

There are many places to get information about your town: library, chamber of commerce, city hall or civic center, churches and synagogues, museums, a college or university, or your local historical society. Ask someone at school. Ask older people in the community what they remember. They will help you reconstruct the past with books, pictures, and maps. You will see how manmade and natural features came and disappeared, and how names came to be.

When you have done your research, compare the newest and oldest maps of the area. Do you recognize your hometown?

4 DIVIDING THE WORLD

You started with your own familiar corner of the world. You know how to draw it and how to get around in it.

How about the world? How do you divide up our earth so that it can be shown on a map?

A map is flat, but the world is round. The best way to map a round world—a globe—is **on** a globe. For instance, a globe shows us that most of the land is in the northern part of the world and most of the water in the south. Such a map is the only way we can see everything in its real position in relation to everywhere else. A globe shows the world in miniature, in perspective, and in true scale.

But a globe, though an accurate map, has several drawbacks. It would have to be enormous to show any kind of detail. The Daily News Building in New York City has the largest globe in the world, with a diameter of twelve feet. Not even that globe can show us the details we need. Hundreds of different globes are needed—to show, for example,

rainfall or population or crops. A globe can't be folded neatly into your pocket. Although in the eighteenth century globes were so fashionable that pocket-size ones were made, each with its own case. The pockets must have been very large. . . .

Globes have only limited use as maps, but they do remind us that the earth is round. It isn't perfectly round, though. The centrifugal force created by the earth's great speed of rotation (1,038 miles per hour) makes the earth actually a **spheroid**—its circular shape slightly flattened at the North and South Pole and slightly bulging at the equator. The earth is also tilted on its axis—the imaginary line drawn between the poles. It is tilted at an angle of 23½° as it makes its orbit around the sun. And while globes show the tilt of the earth, a flat map cannot.

There is neither beginning nor end to a sphere or a circle, but to divide it in order to make a framework for maps you have to start somewhere. The ancient Babylonians, who were great mathematicians, divided the year into 360 days. So, similarly, they divided the circle of the world into 360 sections called degrees—the way it is on your compass. Each degree represents a portion of the whole globe.

We divide the globe into 360° in two ways: horizontally and vertically using two sets of **coordinates.** The horizontal coordinates are the **parallels of latitude.** These measure distance on the earth north and south of the equator, the base line. The **equator** is a giant, imaginary ring circling the earth at its widest part, halfway between the North and South Poles. The parallel of latitude of the equator is zero degrees. The imaginary lines of latitude circling the world are parallel—never meeting the equator or each other. They go in ever smaller circles until they reach the poles at 90°N and 90°S.

Parallels of latitude

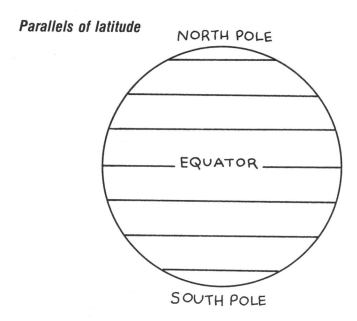

NORTH POLE

EQUATOR

SOUTH POLE

Halfway between the equator and the North Pole, at a latitude of 45°N, is the Tropic of Cancer. Halfway between the equator and the South Pole, at 45°S, is the Tropic of Capricorn.

Each degree of latitude covers 69 miles, and each degree in turn is divided into 60 minutes—and the minutes subdivided into 60 seconds. The latitude of Summertown is 42 degrees, 15 minutes,

25 seconds north (42° 15′ 25″N). This kind of detail can pinpoint the latitude of any spot on the globe to within 100 feet.

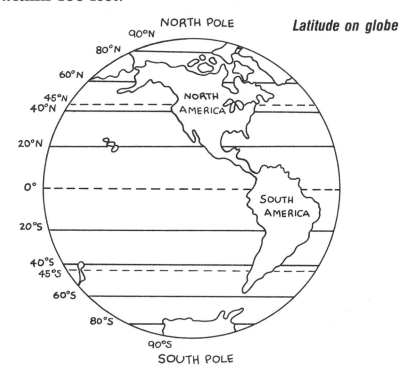

Latitude on globe

People have known how to work out latitude since the time of the ancient Greeks. **Astrolabes, quadrants,** and **sextants** are optical instruments used for the necessary sightings and calculations. Navigators measure the angle between the horizon and the sun at midday, or the horizon and the North Star in the northern half of the world at night. Tables are then used to tell the distance of a place north or south of the equator—its latitude—if the sun is a certain number of degrees above the horizon at noon on a particular date.

The vertical coordinates on a globe are called **meridians of longitude**. They circle the globe from north to south, meeting at the poles and crossing the parallels of latitude at right angles. Meridians of longitude measure east-west distances on the

Meridians of longitude

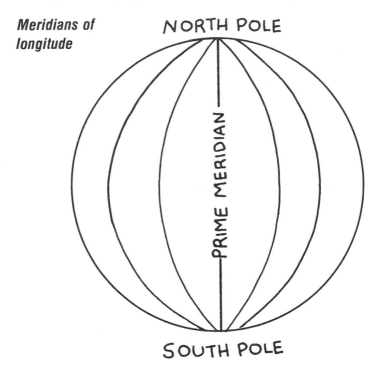

NORTH POLE

PRIME MERIDIAN

SOUTH POLE

earth. But east of what? West of what? There is no east or west pole. For a long time no one could measure east-west distances. A base line was needed, somewhere to start calculations from. In 1884, it was decided to use the meridian that passed through Greenwich, England, as the base line or **prime meridian.** Greenwich was marked at zero degrees. We count 90° west or 90° east from Greenwich around the world. But how much east or west?

Longitude is divided and measured by time—the time it takes the earth to complete a revolution. The sun appears to move 15° of the 360° in one hour, and so longitude is normally measured in 15° divisions around the globe, although it can be measured in 20° and other divisions. People couldn't accurately measure these time divisions until a **chronometer,** a reliable timepiece, was invented. A chronometer could be set to prime meridian time—and would keep it accurately even on board a ship. In 1735, John Harrison made such a chronometer. Today, the radio keeps us accurately informed about time.

Measuring longitude works like this: Say you

Longitude on globe

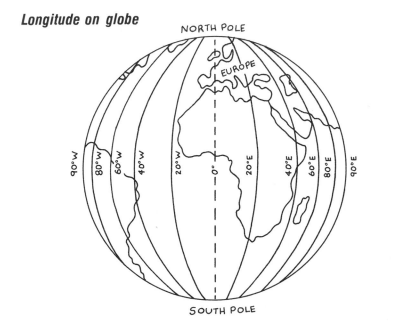

33

are in the middle of the Atlantic Ocean without radio contact. It is high noon by the sun. The chronometer, set to prime meridian time, says 3 P.M., so the time difference between you and 0° at Greenwich is three hours. Your distance, therefore, is three hours west of Greenwich, although it may have taken many more hours to get there. One hour is 15°. 15 × 3 = 45. Your longitude is 45°W. You can pinpoint exactly where you are by calculating latitude and longitude. (Convention always puts latitude first.) The position of Summertown is $42°15'25"N$ (latitude), and $71°45'15"W$ (longitude)—a very exact spot.

The distance covered by one degree of longitude is not constant, as latitude is. Parallels of latitude are equal distances from each other and therefore the distance covered by each degree is always the same. One degree of longitude measures 69 miles at the equator, but meridians of longitude gradually come together at the poles. Therefore, as you go toward the poles, the distance between the meridians lessens until all lines meet.

You might think that where the two zeros of latitude and longitude meet would be somewhere important: London or Washington, or at least a glamorous place like Acapulco or Bali. Actually it is a lonely spot of water some 400 miles west of central Africa.

When you draw both the lines of latitude and longitude, you have the basic grid or network of coordinates for the world. This makes the framework or skeleton for a map, indicating north, south, east, and west for everywhere on earth.

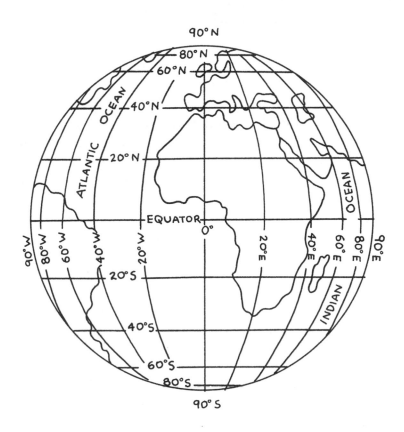

Grid/network on globe

5 PROJECTING THE WORLD

It is a pity that our ancestors were wrong in thinking the world was flat. A flat world is easily represented on flat paper. How do you make a sphere flat and still keep the original features and proportions accurate? Try it. Get an old hollow rubber ball and cut it up so you can put the whole thing flat on the table. How did you do the cutting? Did you keep it all in on piece or make orange slice sections? Does it lie flat? Maybe you had to cheat a bit to make it stay flat—stretch a little here, squash a little there.

Cartographers—mapmakers—have the same problem. The round world is put on flat paper by **projecting** it. Projections are mathematical ways of flattening out the sphere of the earth and putting it, together with its network of coordinates, on paper. In other words, projecting is changing from three dimensions to two. All projections have to be distortions; they are just various ways of looking at the world.

The most familiar way of looking at the world is **Mercator's projection**. We have become so used to seeing the world this way that we don't realize what a distorted view it is. It is only really accurate around the equator. The farther north and south you look, the less true the map is. There are no poles at all. Africa is split so that one half is at the right of the map and the other half at the left. Greenland, at the top of the map, is way out of proportion; it is nowhere near as big as it looks. The Antarctic stretches gigantically across the bottom.

The reason for the distortion is that Mercator's

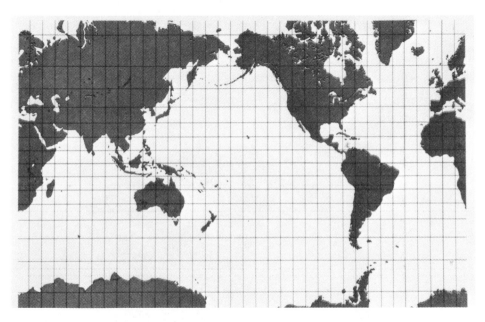

Mercator's projection

projection is a rectangle in which all the meridians of longitude are vertical and set equal intervals apart. The parallels of latitude cross at right angles, making small rectangles inside the big rectangle—Mercator's "signature."

All compass directions on Mercator's map are

straight lines. Mercator created his projection to simplify navigating at sea. But other shapes can also be projected as flat maps. For example, the **Lambert conic projection** shows an area of the globe as a cone, which can be sliced into shapes. The projection is good for wide, east-to-west lands like the United States.

Mapmakers can also decide to center a projection on a specific point on the globe and draw radiating great circles from it. The **polar projection** focuses on the North or South Pole. You can also center the world on Bangkok or Denver or Summertown.

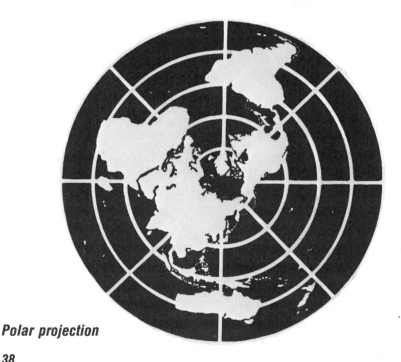

Polar projection

It is perfectly possible to make a map of the world by flattening the whole thing out, as you would flatten out the peel of an orange. You simply have spaces in the map. These sections are called **gores**, which can be glued onto a globe or made into a flat map. **Goode's interrupted projection** uses gores to emphasize the world's land areas, or the ocean areas if "interrupted" another way.

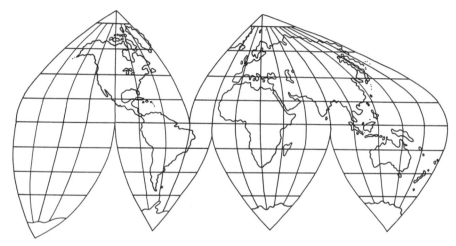

Goode's interrupted projection emphasizing the world's land areas

Every map is to a certain extent an imaginary vision of the world. You have to decide what you want or need most in a map, what you are using a particular map for, and what properties you look for. Do you want the shape to look like the real thing? You can do it in small areas when you conform to shape in a **conformal** map like Mercator's.

Navigators, engineers, builders, and soldiers need conformal maps.

Do you need to compare one place with another—the size of Oregon compared with the size of Florida? You need a map in scale, in proportion to the area it represents, an **equal-area** map like the **Albers conic.** An acre on one map must be an acre on another. You need this kind of map also to show statistics—how many people, cows, goldmines, or whatever. The resulting maps may look pulled out of shape, but so long as you cover the right amount of space, the shape of the space doesn't matter. The important point is, whichever projection is used, each place must be kept at the exact crossing of its coordinates—at its true location.

There is no best projection. Each distorts the earth in a different way. But each has its special usefulness.

6 WORLD ALMOST IN YOUR POCKET

While it might be technically possible to put most of the factual information available about the world on a single and enormous map, the result would be chaotic to the eye. It is more satisfactory to divide the world into many separate maps, each of which emphasizes different characteristics. Those separate maps are collected into a book of maps called an **atlas**.

An atlas is usually arranged so that it starts with a bird's-eye view of the whole world seen from all sides, including the top and bottom polar regions. These views are followed by separate views of the continents. Each continent is followed by the individual countries comprising it. Units, such as Scandinavia, are also given. Sometimes even smaller divisions are included: the area around capital cities or groups of islands. The country publishing the atlas usually shows its own subdivisions in detail. A United States atlas, for instance, will show the individual states.

Maps in an atlas belong to two basic groups. The first group shows the natural features of the earth, the land and water areas. These are **physical** maps. Natural features can be shown by color and **relief**. Relief means the variations in height of the land surface and surfaces beneath the sea. This relief map of Scandinavia clearly shows the massive mountains, low-lying plains with scattered lakes, and the rivers running almost parallel throughout the peninsula. The sharp inlets of the rocky western coastline stand out. Natural color is used for a realistic effect.

How high is high on a relief map? The legend at

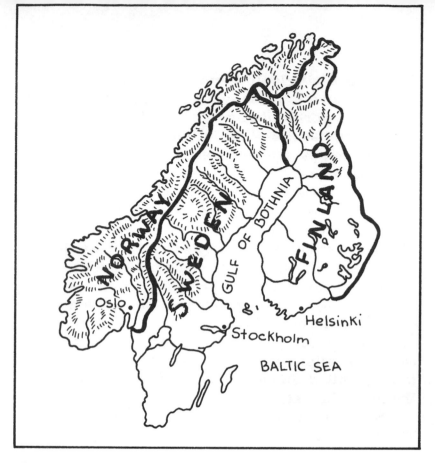

Physical or relief map of Scandinavia

the side of the map explains this by using shades of the same color, grading the color according to height. Height and depth can also be shown by a **profile** or **section drawing** of the area. You already know another way of showing height: the contour lines of a topographical map.

Physical maps can also show what the interior of the earth is made of—its **geology**.

The other basic map group is the **regional** or

political. These maps show cities, boundaries, and the uses we make of the earth's surface for things like farming, mining, and irrigation. These maps look more cluttered than physical ones because they are full of names.

Special-purpose regional maps are mainly divided into agriculture, industry, and natural resources. They often also show population, rainfall, temperature, and vegetation. Special-purpose maps often conserve space by using the same map for different kinds of facts. Industry and natural resources can be differentiated by symbols and color. Only the law of clarity governs what should be included, and how to do it.

There is some overlapping between physical and regional maps. Some physical maps show cities. Regional maps can show important physical features to allow readers to orient themselves.

Regional maps are **planimetric**, which means they are flat, without contours or other attempts to show height. Topographical and other physical maps are characterized by their ability to show height.

Some atlases are concerned with specific subjects, like maps of places in history or in the Bible. And there are other books of maps that are not atlases: road maps, town charts, tourist guides, and coastal maps.

Coastal maps are called **charts**. They use scale and projections and show direction like any other map, but the information they contain is for the navigator and sailor.

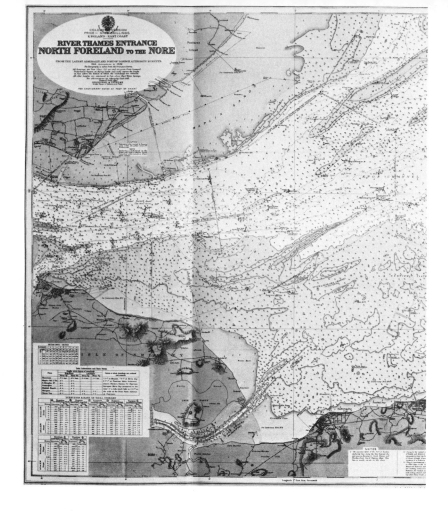

Coastal marine chart

Charts show the shapes and characteristics of coastlines, whether rocky promontories or smooth sand beaches. Useful landmarks are shown, including warnings of danger: lighthouses, lightships, buoys. The dangers themselves—rocks, reefs, wrecks—are also shown. The direction and force of winds, tides, and currents are given. What is at the bottom of the water is taken into account: mud, sand, rock, and the depth of the water, particularly in harbors and difficult channels. The ocean depth is given at the average low tide for the area and is stated in fathoms. One fathom equals six feet.

The maps in an atlas are shown as accurately as possible, choosing the most suitable projection for each. But the reader would never be able to figure out if a country like Iceland was bigger or smaller than Australia, if it weren't for scale. You found out about scale when you drew your sketch map and when you used the topographical map for your hike. Scale in an atlas is also a yardstick of importance, because a country of renowned international stature will be shown on a large scale with all kinds of detail, even if it is physically very small.

The rule is simple: small-scale maps usually cover large areas (1:10,000,000 is small scale). And large scale maps cover small areas. (The maps on pp. 2, 3 and 4 show the difference in scale.) Scale is stated in several ways. The **representative fraction** or **RF** is one way. For instance, 1:62,500 or 1/62,500 means that one inch on the map equals approximately one mile on the ground (1:63,360 exactly equals one mile). That was the scale you used on the hike. You can also put scale in words on the map legend: "One inch equals one mile." Or you can use a bar scale like a ruler:

Bar scale

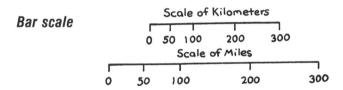

In addition to color, and various ways of showing height and depth, mapmakers save space and strive for clarity by using an agreed-upon system, a **convention**, of symbols. These are abstract and realistic pictures, and various combinations of dotted and lined patterns. They are explained in the key or legend at the side. You have to take into account the meaning of a particular symbol. A dot on one map may mean a town of 25,000 people. The same dot on another map may mean a city of 2 million. Or the dot may mean 100 head of cattle. Always check how the legend translates the dot. Once you understand the symbols, you can read the map.

Design and style are important to maps, so long as clarity is not sacrificed for art. Lettering, printing, and color are what add style to a map. The end result should be pleasing to the eye, clear and uncluttered, and tell you what you want to know. A confusing, badly thought out, or badly drawn map is worse than none at all.

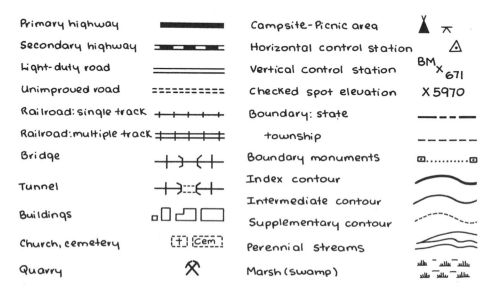

Selected topographical map symbols, U.S. Geological Survey

Much information in addition to the actual maps goes into an atlas. Often there is an introduction with diagrams of the evolution of the world, its environment, and its position in space. In the body of the atlas there may be capsuled information about the various countries. Near each regional map will be a list of places shown on that map. At the back of the atlas is a **gazetteer**, an informative index, often listing places not included on the actual map. Population figures are often given for each place. The reference to the place's location in the atlas can be given by page number, possibly by latitude and longitude, or by grid number.

Certain other facts go into atlases that are important for the map user to be aware of. Always make sure to check the date of the atlas. When was it published? The world never stops changing, and atlases become outdated very quickly. They can be outdated the moment they are printed. Maybe a revolution or a war gave country A to country B, or countries C and D merged. After World War I and again after World War II, the whole map of Europe changed. Britain altered its county plan in 1974, and so the subdivisions of the country changed. The map of Africa has changed many times, partly due to the creation of new countries.

Everywhere airports are constructed, railroads extended or abandoned, highways built, harbors expanded. Cities grow or shrink. Physical maps change because of the natural stresses and forces of the earth. In 1883, a tremendous volcanic explosion blew up most of the island of Krakatoa and changed the shape of the strait between Java and Sumatra. The ash and lava that poured out created new islands. In 1963, also as a result of volcanic activity, an entirely new island, Surtsey, appeared off the coast of Iceland. Volcanoes themselves change in height every time they erupt. Other forces cause deserts to spread, rivers to change course or dry up.

Place names also change. The city of St. Petersburg became Petrograd and then Leningrad. Leopoldville became Kinshasa. Whole countries change their names: the Gold Coast became Ghana, Rhodesia became Zimbabwe. Sometimes only the spelling of a name changes, as in the new Chinese spelling system: for instance, the city of Peking is now Beijing.

Atlases keep as up to date as possible by using the latest census information and surveys of various kinds. The editors obtain statistics from yearbooks and other recurring information sources.

There are other influences at work, too. Where was your atlas produced? Is it objective or biased? It is natural and sensible for a country to give plenty of space to show different aspects of its own territory. But if it makes certain things more attractive by, for example, using cheerful colors and bold lettering, and downgrades other countries by showing them in muddy, depressing tones and small print, it is biased.

Why call a book of maps an atlas? In Greek mythology, Atlas was a Titan who tried to dethrone Zeus, the king of the gods. For his audacity he was doomed to carry the sky on his shoulders forever to prevent it from falling on the world.

7 SMALL WORLD

We are used to maps filled with information, and we trust them to show the world as it is. Yet it has taken much of humanity's existence to put the whole world on paper in this familiar way we take for granted.

The earliest maps of all were like your neighborhood sketch map. People started by drawing a picture of their nearest surroundings, to indicate where they lived and to show others. One's home, the center of one's life and world, went in the middle of the map. For centuries the most important local place was automatically the center of the map.

The oldest maps that still exist date back over 2,000 years and come from the Middle East— Babylon and Egypt. Marked on clay tablets, they show city plans and indicate property ownership. People thought that the world was flat and saw that it obviously extended beyond the horizon, but they didn't know how far. They were sure it couldn't be very far, and equally sure that the surface of the world came to an end in ocean in whichever direction they looked. Beyond the ocean there was probably nothing, and one would most likely fall off the edge of the world.

The first map we have of what was considered to be the whole world is from the sixth century B.C. The "world" consists of Babylon—in the center, of course—and its neighboring countries, surrounded by sea. It was a small, flat disc of a world, accurately drawn only in the local areas the mapmakers knew. The rest was unknown, even though the Middle Easterners belonged to advanced civilizations.

The ancient Chinese also worked out what the world looked like from their point of view, but the knowledge they had and the maps they drew did not reach the rest of the world.

Ignorance, with a brief, shining, and eventually far-reaching exception, continued for century after dark century, until after the Middle Ages. The exception was Greece. With their mathematics and science, their philosophy and sheer common sense, the Greeks worked out a system they called **geography**, meaning "writing about the earth." Much of it is still in use today.

First of all, the Greeks realized the earth was a sphere and not flat. And they mathematically worked out an accurate measurement of the earth and its circumference, even though no one had traveled the whole way around it. The Greeks gave us the equator and the Tropics of Cancer and Capricorn, which they worked out from astronomical observations. In addition to these parallels of latitude, they thought out the idea of meridians and the tilt and rotation of the earth.

Unfortunately, there are no Greek maps for us to examine.

The Romans came after the Greeks. They traveled extensively over the world, conquering and civilizing. They drew maps for their expeditions, but only a few fragments have survived as evidence.

This scarcity of maps has been a problem throughout the ages. Maps are meant to be used, so they wear out, fall apart, get thrown away, are lost at sea or on arduous treks, or are destroyed as secret documents, often in wartime. Many were single copies—once lost, gone forever.

The peak of ancient mapmaking was reached by Ptolemy at Alexandria in Egypt in the second century A.D. He wrote the first scientifically researched book on geography, appropriately called **Geography**. He brought together all that was known of past and current information. He did it so systematically and well that his work was the standard reference book until the sixteenth century. The **Geography** contained many maps, using the equal-area projection Ptolemy had invented. He used coordinates and scale in his maps and included a great many place names.

Ptolemy made several errors, however, and for a long time they were not corrected. Even when it was known that they **were** errors, they were so firmly fixed in people's thinking that it was extremely difficult to get rid of them. Ptolemy miscalculated the size of the earth, thinking it smaller than it is. On the other hand, he said that the continent of Asia was even more enormous than it is, extending much farther into the Pacific Ocean. He showed China as simply extending east off the map. This mistake was the main reason seafarers thought it would be relatively easy and quick to sail westward to China from Europe. It seemed to be not that far away.

These ideas were dangerous enough. However, Ptolemy had another idea that was incorrect in a different way. He decided—against the earlier Greek theories—that the earth was the center of its universe; it stood still while the sun revolved around it. When later astronomers such as Copernicus and Galileo tried to tell the truth—that the earth revolves around the sun—they were not believed. Once in people's minds and on maps, Ptolemy's errors, and those of other early geographers, persisted.

This capacity for the survival of errors was doubly strange, because all the good work that the Greeks and Ptolemy himself had done was lost without a trace for over a thousand years, as if it had never existed.

In the Dark Ages, the great library at Alexandria in Egypt was burned to the ground by invaders. Alexandria was the greatest center of the known world's culture, and its library contained practically all the knowledge that had been gathered up to that time. When the library was burned in 391 A.D., all the thousands of books, including Ptolemy's, went with it.

Ptolemy's map of the world, about 150 A.D.

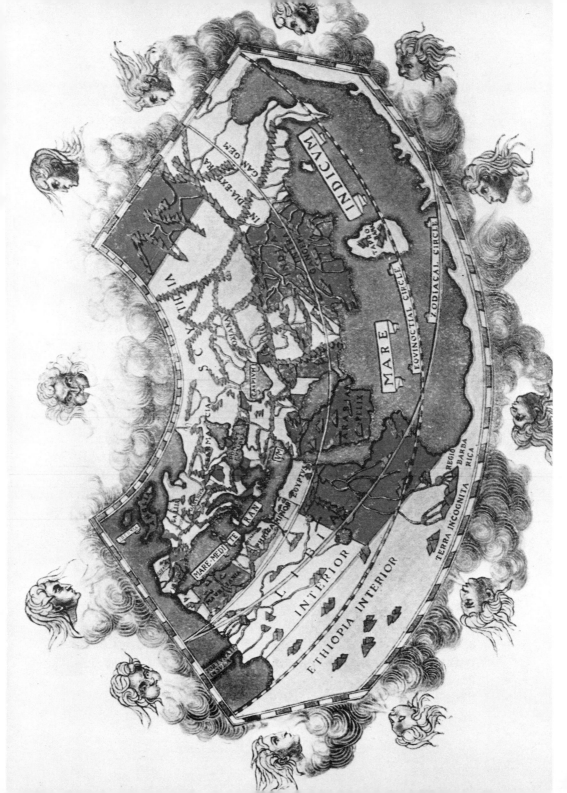

Some people felt that books were against religion. Therefore, strong religious beliefs kept much of the Western world from new learning for centuries.

The decline and fall of the Roman Empire in the fourth and fifth centuries A.D. left Europe open to barbarian conquest. Only small pockets of learning existed, mainly in monasteries. But the learning was not scientific. The people of the Dark and Middle Ages distrusted anything new.

A few practical maps were drawn, mainly sketch maps showing pilgrims the way to shrines, but most maps were nothing more than detailed and beautiful pictures. These maps mixed religion, myths, and tall stories and were filled with fear of the unknown.

Religious leaders said Jerusalem was the most important place on earth, so Jerusalem was placed in the middle of the map. Paradise was in the east because the Bible said so, and though no one knew exactly where it was, it went on the map. All medieval maps put east at the top, toward heaven. There was a great deal about the world that people didn't know, so the pictures were filled out with imaginary places, and with monsters and saints and mythical creatures.

Probably the best medieval picture map in existence is the one at Hereford Cathedral in England. The Hereford map is a work of art, drawn on vellum—a writing surface made from calf-skin—and full of color and gold leaf. Like all medieval "maps," it is useless as a map. But it is an encyclo-

pedia of people's beliefs and knowledge in the late
thirteenth century. The mapmaker was visually

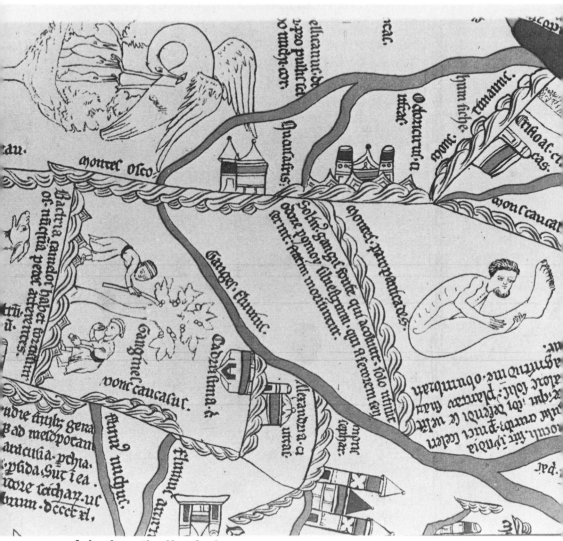

Asia, from the Hereford map

explaining the world to a population that couldn't read, a world of Bible stories, strange creatures, and weird people. Asia is shown at the top (eastern) part of the map, the known part of Africa is on the right (south). Europe is unrecognizably at the bottom left, with the Mediterranean in the middle, packed with islands. The Day of Judgment dominates the map, to remind people that this world was only a way station to the next.

Fantasy is hard to erase. Even in the seventeenth century, a Dutch map with trustworthy parallels of latitude and detailed marine information,

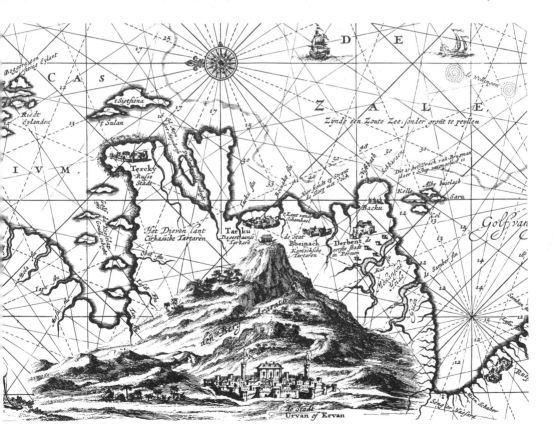

Map of the Caspian Sea with Mt. Ararat, and ark

shows a little Noah's ark at the top of Mount Ararat. The biblical ark was supposed to have landed there after the flood.

During the Middle Ages, travel to the East increased, but this was not reflected in the storytelling maps. Maps were made indoors, not in the field. On the Hereford map, a river separates England from Scotland. The mapmakers could have gone to see for themselves that this was not so, but they didn't. However, harbor, coastal, and sea-route charts continued to be accurately produced, mainly by chartmakers living near the Mediterranean Sea. These charts show the first extensive use of the magnetic compass. The compass turned people's minds to observation, common sense, and facts. Use of the compass also meant that—gradually—maps began to be reoriented to the north.

The invention of the printing press in Europe in the mid-fifteenth century meant that books could be produced in greater numbers than possible when

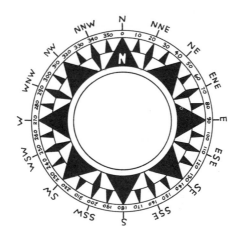

Compass rose—called that because it looks like a stylized flower. A mariner's compass that shows wind directions instead of, or in addition to, the 360° of travel directions.

they had to be hand copied. Books appeared on a variety of subjects, and after a thousand years, Ptolemy's **Geography** was rediscovered. The only problem was that Ptolemy was then treated with as much reverence as the Bible itself. What he stated was considered gospel truth, including his errors.

Fortunately, the rebirth of learning and the dawning of the great age of discovery were changing the world. This rebirth, the Renaissance, meant that inquiring minds and scientific methods were on the rise, even though there was still much reliance on classical antiquity. Monsters could be eliminated from maps to make room for reality. People began to expand their vision, to explore the world. And they drew what they actually saw and measured it as well as they could. Maps began to look more like the ones we use today.

8 *GROWING WORLD*

Ptolemy's maps had a powerful influence on Christopher Columbus. Like everyone else, Columbus believed in Ptolemy's vast, eastern-extending China. The overland route east to the lands of spices and other luxuries had been traveled by hardy souls, such as Marco Polo, a hundred years before Columbus. However, political changes and religious differences among people made the route by land even more dangerous than before. For all practical purposes, that way was closed. And the route eastward by sea was long, hard, and beset by pirates.

The major countries that were doing all the exploration and colonization—Spain, Portugal, and England—began to look westward. They thought there was nothing but ocean beyond the British Isles all the way to China. No one knew just how far that was. Ships were small and had limited supplies of food and water.

Columbus, working for the Spanish king, researched all there was to know in history and geography books, especially Ptolemy's work, about a possible western route. He calculated that he could make the journey and land in China or Japan. When he landed in the West Indies, he naturally thought he was in Asia—all the calculations said so. No one could have known that Asia was so much farther away that a whole continent—the Americas—and a whole ocean—the Pacific—were in between. The wildest dreams of medieval mapmakers hadn't imagined that.

Columbus was a good mapmaker. But on his second voyage, he took with him Juan de la Cosa, who was an even better mapmaker. Juan de la Cosa was the first person to put what would soon be called the Americas on the map. He painted the world on an oxhide chart in 1500. America—not then named—was part of China and consisted of the West Indies, the northern part of South America, and a vague outline reaching up to Labrador. Only the coastlines were shown.

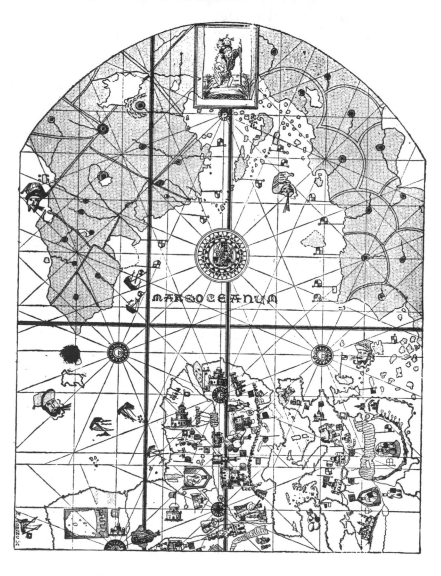

MARE OCEANUM

Map by Juan de la Cosa, pilot to Christopher Columbus on his second voyage. The dark patches are North and South America.

By the mid-sixteenth century, much of the New World coastline, east and west, began to be known. But California was a question mark on the maps for a century. Was it an island or not? Even after it was known to be connected to the mainland, it was often still shown on new maps as separate.

Ponce de Leon discovered Florida and thought it was an island, too. British explorers such as Henry Hudson, Sir Martin Frobisher, and Sir Walter Raleigh, and the Venetian John Cabot who worked for England, also extended the map of America as they sought a passage to China.

The interior of America was then **terra incognita**—unknown land—so the empty space was still occasionally filled with nonexistent scenery by mapmakers. The empty center was also a good place for the **cartouche**, the medallion containing the name of the map and the dedication. Maps were usually dedicated to the person who put up the money for their production. The cartouche was elaborately lettered, worded, and decorated.

During the sixteenth and seventeenth centuries, most of our world was discovered. Ferdinand Magellan proved the world was navigable all the way around, and showed there was a way—a long way—to China by sailing around the tip of South America.

Exploring and mapmaking now were closely related. There was much more to put on maps. And there was a matching surge in the technical skills of mapmaking and map publishing. The financial climate was right. Money was available for travel, discovery, settlement, new foreign trade, and, therefore, maps.

From 1500 onward, the Italians and then the Flemish and especially the Portuguese and Dutch—all great sailors and merchants—developed mapmaking on a large commercial scale. They improved skills in the related arts of papermaking and illustrating in woodcuts and engravings. The advantage of woodcuts and engravings was that copies could be made in large numbers. Copper engraving, carried out especially in the Netherlands, produced finer lines and more details than could be made in woodcuts.

Maps tended to be large, and not many people had the space for them. Folded-up maps, with their accompanying texts, in book form made bulky objects. This was a big problem for the brilliant mapmaker Martin Waldseemüller of Germany. He was the man who first called the New World "America," taken from the name of a contemporary Italian explorer, Amerigo Vespucci. The explorer had recently discovered that South America was separate from Asia, and Waldseemüller was the first to give the name to the whole continent on his world map of 1507.

Gerardus Mercator and Abraham Ortelius, Flemish geographers, solved the problem of bulky collections of maps and texts. Mercator collected his own projections in what he called an "atlas," in three volumes, in 1538. His maps showed a northwest passage to the Far East through the top of North America. But finding this passage was a continuing challenge to explorers who discovered many other lands instead, opening North America to colonization.

Ortelius's approach to his atlas was different from Mercator's. Ortelius collected maps from all possible sources, engraved them on sheets of paper of the same size, and bound them together in a book. Large maps were divided to fit on several pages, or mathematically reduced in size. His **Theater of the World**, published in 1570, was the first modern atlas. Beautifully engraved and colored, the top of his world map shows a broad highway of a northwest passage. The bottom shows a vast southern continent "not yet discovered," which everyone believed extended just south of South America.

Other map publishers followed the examples of Mercator and Ortelius, making beautiful engravings of maps, developing the use of color and shading, and trying different ways of showing hills and rivers. There were different schools of thought and ideas in different countries. The Dutch and British, for example, liked to include inserts of towns or areas, and the French didn't.

When looking at old maps, you can see what people looked for in a map in earlier days. John Speed's **Atlas of Tudor England and Wales** of 1627 shows that era's interest in productivity. The goods produced on the land and also the method of transporting them via river are predominant on the map.

Seventeenth-century cartographers and map publishers kept the standard of map production at a high level as new lands were discovered. The public was fascinated and needed only to have the word "new" added to a map to buy it.

Beginning in the mid-seventeenth century, scientific inquiry dominated and many mysteries and misunderstandings about the physical nature of the world were cleared up. Sir Isaac Newton worked out his theory of gravity and centrifugal force. He and his contemporaries calculated the shape of the earth much more accurately than before and proved it to be a spheroid, not a sphere. This knowledge is basic to **geodesy**, which is the mathematical calculation of the real shape and size of the earth, not counting its superficial heights of mountains and depths of ocean trenches. The framework of any accurate map is based on geodetic calculations.

New facts about the world went hand in hand with the development and improvement of instruments and tools for studying it. Better telescopes advanced astronomy, making heavenly—and earthly—calculations more accurate.

With fewer places left to explore, interest grew in the content—the details—of what had been discovered. People realized they had to go outside to measure and map the actual land. They had to **survey** it. Surveying is related to geodesy, on a smaller scale. Surveyors find out the shape, size, and position of a piece of land by using various measurement tools and geometry. The idea of surveying was not new. People recognized that places had to have limits and not wander vaguely off the map into nothing.

To survey something, you start with a base line. This base line is accurately measured using a special chain or tape. Nowadays we measure lines with electronic instruments such as the **geodimeter**, which uses light waves, or the **tellurometer**, which uses radio waves, or with **laser beams**, which are narrow beams of light. Then the **theodolite**, a telescope mounted on a tripod, is used to measure the angles between the base line and a specific point. That point is joined to each end of the base line to create a triangle. This is the basis of **triangulation**, which is the only way to keep a straight line over the curved surface of the earth. Each triangle is mathematically based on the last. The starting triangle for the United States was measured in a field at Meades Ranch in Kansas in 1927—the very center of America. The network spreads out from there to include the whole country.

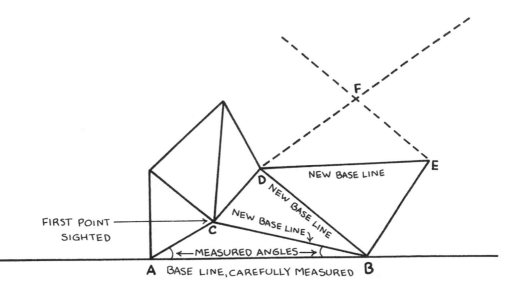

Triangulation diagram

Control points showing heights are placed around the country. They are round or triangular, made of metal, and set in concrete for stability. You may come across one in a city, on the beach, or in the hills. You can be certain to see one at the highest point of local terrain. A control point looks like this:

Control point. This one shows vertical position above sea level and is called a benchmark. Horizontal markers show latitude and longitude of specific positions.

In the eighteenth century, France led the world in national surveying. The surveys were mapped and became a model for other countries, such as Great Britain. The British government's Ordnance Survey started in 1791 and ended fifty years later.

Captain James Cook, an explorer and map-maker, was England's very best surveyor. He surveyed the coasts of Newfoundland and Labrador with great accuracy. He circumnavigated the globe and disproved the myth of an undiscovered southern continent. Cook mapped much of the Southern Hemisphere that **was** there, in the Pacific and Antarctic Oceans. He also carried out extensive coastal surveys of New Zealand and Australia.

Most of the outlines of the world and the interiors of comparatively small areas like Great Britain and France had been mapped as well as explored by the nineteenth century. Now the large interiors of continents had to be systematically surveyed. Explorers, of course, mapped where they had been, but their work was disjointed and sketchy.

Surveyors, wherever they went, had to be tough, and good explorers, too. The surveying of America included three-mile-high mountains, seemingly endless plains, deserts, swamps, and every extreme of temperature.

Some of the most important boundary lines in America were established at the very beginning of colonial days. They were the dividing lines of royal grants to settlers in the original colonies and territories. Surveying in those times was an almost necessary knowledge, as well as an honorable profession for the gentleman settler building a large estate. George Washington studied surveying, and Thomas Jefferson was the son of a surveyor.

The Mason-Dixon line, symbol of the division of north and south in the United States, was originally drawn to clarify the boundary between the British colonies of Pennsylvania and Maryland, and was the starting point for surveying the country.

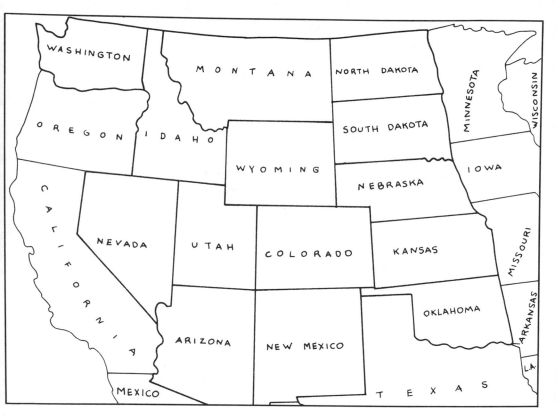

Rectangular states of America's heartland

The General Land Office (later called the Bureau of Land Management) was the original governmental surveying and mapping office. When the government offered public land to pioneers going

West, the Land Office surveyed and mapped all the land into rectangles. Look at the map. Everything west and south of Ohio is rectangular, with rectangular subdivisions, except where natural lines such as rivers create boundaries.

The Louisiana Purchase in 1803 doubled the territory of the United States. The government sponsored the Lewis and Clark expedition from 1804-1806 to explore the new territory. The expedition followed the Missouri, Snake, and Columbia rivers to the Pacific coast and back. An enormous amount of information was added to the map of the interior of America and opened the West to settlement.

By the mid-nineteenth century, there were many maps of the West and the West Coast compiled from various surveys and explorations. The opening up of the Colorado River territory produced another vast area to be mapped.

In 1879, the U.S. Geological Survey was founded to centralize, standardize, and map all the information that had been collected about the vast continent. The result was the basis for the system of maps of different scales, types, and purposes that we use today. You used one type of map on that hike in New Hampshire; it is the American version of the British Ordnance Survey.

The early nineteenth century saw the invention of a new printing technique that was quickly brought into use for producing commercial maps—**lithography**. It was a quick, inexpensive, and effective method that gradually replaced engraving, though it was less attractive to look at. At the same time, the use of contour lines replaced earlier methods for showing height, such as pictures of hills or shading called hachuring, which looked like bushy eyebrows.

Roads and railroads took up more of the countryside and more of the map as a result. Symbols and other map conventions became increasingly important as room on the map decreased. Art has vanished from the map, but conciseness, accuracy, precision, and objectivity are beautiful qualities that we look for in maps today.

9 THE WORLD KNOWN

The whole world, except for Antarctica, had been mapped in some way by the end of the nineteenth century. And the whole world wanted to be in on the mapping adventure. International committees set up world standards for mapmaking. For instance, they decided on one prime meridian, at Greenwich instead of those used at various other times. They agreed on symbols, and the exact length of a meter and a mile.

There were also efforts to produce a very accurate and practical international world map on a scale of 1:1,000,000 (one to a million) using metric measure. Called the Millionth Map, it was a very ambitious project—so ambitious that we're still at it.

Even so, at the beginning of the twentieth century only one-ninth of the globe had been accurately surveyed. And mapping methods, though improved, were still agonizingly slow, relying on human feet and stamina. It took World War I (1914-1918) to get surveying and mapmaking off the ground and into the twentieth century with two developments: the airplane and improved photographic techniques.

Aerial photography made it possible for people to get records of what they could see without actually going there. This was the beginning of our many **remote sensing** techniques. Aerial photography didn't produce completed maps (See the aerial photograph of Brooklyn on p. 26.) The plane flew in parallel tracks, each one covering some of the previous territory, producing a series of overlapping pictures so that nothing was missed. Photographs taken at an angle, however, give a distorted view. And if terrain is photographed looking straight down, everything below looks flat.

Photographs had to be converted to maps. A simple **photo map** is an aerial photograph to which map data—such as symbols—have been added. **Aerial maps** are assembled from the middle and best part of each photo. Various instruments are then used to transform the information into clear maps.

A **stereoscope** makes objects on the ground appear to be three-dimensional. The scene is then magnified, and a precise map, including relief, can be compiled. This map is then photochemically reproduced on the plastic sheets now used for maps.

Airplanes are useful for helping to map the earth. And pilots also need their own kinds of maps for flying. Air charts show flight paths, airports, radio communication networks, and the location of radio stations. Showing variations in land heights is essential—no one wants to fly into a mountain. Skyscrapers are marked in cities because no one wants to fly into them, either. Also marked on air charts are sensitive areas—where it is forbidden to fly over for reasons of safety, security, or just noise prevention—in this and other countries.

Aerial photography didn't work when the area was covered by clouds, fog, or deep shadow. For a long time, this was a major problem, until another method of remote sensing was invented: **radar**. Radar pictures are produced by bouncing radio signals off the terrain. The echoes that return are recorded into images. Radar "sees" through barriers and also shows relief well.

Radar is a kind of electromagnetic energy. This energy moves in waves of different lengths, and each wavelength is good for providing information about some aspect of the world. We try to acquire this kind of information as much as possible, especially using **infrared** wavelengths. Long-wave infrared pictures give us knowledge we could never have before. They can tell, for example, how well a farmer's crops are doing. Since infrared shows up evidence of heat, it is good for mapping volcanic terrain or hot springs, or even for showing the heated buildings of a city.

Spacecraft will be used to a greater degree for mapping in the future. We are using increasingly sophisticated airplane-camera combinations and are adding new technologies—the computer and automation, electronic distance-measuring instruments, and the space sciences.

We can now survey the almost unreachable spots on earth: jungle, snow- and icebound lands like Antarctica, deserts, and oceans. Any two points on earth can be used as the base line in triangulation. A helicopter, an airplane, or an orbiting satellite can be used as the third point of the triangle.

The space program has provided us with another and very different view of our world. The Mercury, Apollo, and Gemini astronauts took pictures of our globe. And inside the spacecraft, a globe is a standard feature to help keep the astronauts oriented.

A program was set up to photograph the earth systematically from space to update our maps, and maps have been quite different as a result. Landsat is a satellite specially created by the National Aeronautics and Space Administration (NASA) to survey the earth from space. Landsat is unmanned and takes computer-controlled-robot photographs from space.

Landsat I was launched in 1973, and since then there have been three more. The latest and most

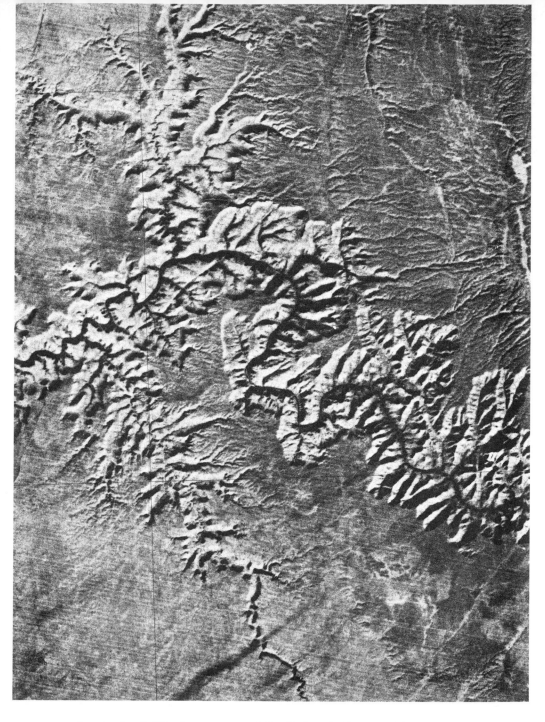

Landsat satellite image map of the Colorado Canyon 1972–3; scale 1:500,000

advanced was sent up in July 1982 and is now the only one in operation. It circles the earth continuously from north to south via the poles, going over the same point on the earth every eighteen days at the same time. Changes that occur over a period of time, like the seasons or crop growth, can be noted and compared.

The Landsat satellite uses two sensor systems: a **multi-spectral scanner**, which transmits information covering 45 square miles per image and gives data in different wavelengths, and a **vidicon**—a kind of TV. Data reach the earth as electronic signals that are recorded on magnetic tape for computer analysis and then conversion to photographlike images. The Landsat imagery is superimposed on a regular map, rather like a photo map. A grid is added with other map information that might be needed.

Landsat images come in black and white, and computer-enhanced **false color**. False color—not the natural colors we are used to—is produced by superimposing three different color images, one over the other, on the black-and-white image. This makes a scene very clear, highlighting healthy vegetation (shown in red), clear water (black), or built-up areas (bluish gray). This imagery is particularly useful for mapping the shape of the land and the kind of vegetation covering it, and for recording urban development. Landsat 4 carries a new gadget, special sensors for **thematic maps**—those with just such particular aims or themes in mind. The thematic mapper reveals more precise detail than the multi-spectral scanner.

The images are useful to naturalists. The Adirondack Park Agency is using Landsat in a variety of ways, such as comparing tree growth with previous years, checking pollution, and monitoring the spread of the gypsy moth. Material that used to take weeks to acquire can now be obtained in a single day. Once the computer equipment is paid for, it is an inexpensive way of gaining information and perspective. But even with this up-to-date equipment a certain amount of on-the-spot checking is necessary, to see, for example, that what looks like swamp isn't really pasture.

Skylab, the manned satellite sent into space in 1973 and '74, orbited at 270 miles above the earth. It provided photographs on film and images on magnetic tape in black and white, color, and false color for scientific experiments, particularly in the areas of land management and planning and conservation. However, the information can be used for just about any purpose requiring mapping. Skylab took photographs of more scattered and limited areas of the world than Landsat, but the pictures are sharper and show more detail.

Satellite observations provide an enormous quantity of geographic information and are vastly increasing our knowledge of the world. We store the information in data banks and use it for research and analysis, planning and education, caring for the environment and all human works in it, and for maps of every conceivable kind. Satellite information is the very latest available, right up to the minute. You can see this every night on your television weather map.

Modern technology has changed the face of the map—the way maps are drawn. It's not very often now that professional cartographers sit down at a large table with just a ruler, a protractor, and a nicely sharpened pencil.

Some maps are still drawn by hand. It is demanding and detailed work, requiring the skills of a careful researcher as well as those of a first-class draftsman. Patience is a necessity—it is not a job that can be rushed. And often the actual drafting of details—roads, symbols, names—is so tiny that cartographers have to use powerful magnifiers to see what they are doing.

Automation and the computer, however, do a lot of our mapmaking now. It is faster and cheaper to have machines do the mechanical chores involved in compiling maps, and machines don't get bored or tired or make mistakes.

Computers can store any kind of information, to be drawn on as needed. Maps can be created on any topic or theme because so much information is instantly available. A basic map can be drawn on a video screen, and the mapmaker, using a keyboard or other means of "writing" on the screen, can add or subtract material. Physical landscapes can be mapped, coordinate/grid systems can be plotted, any projection can be drawn, any type of boundary line inserted. Printouts are available, and often maps can be animated to change as you watch.

Any idea can be made into a map. For instance, how many people wear glasses in the United States? How many people travel by subway in the rush hour in Tokyo? Which towns in the United States with under 30,000 inhabitants mainly vote Republican? What are the statistics of watching Monday Night Football in the Middle Atlantic States? Program your computer, feed in information from your keyboard and look at the data on your video screen. When it tells you all you want, push the button for your hard copy. There is your map, complete and perfect.

10 UNDERWATER WORLD

You could say that the world is really an ocean broken up here and there by pieces of land. Nearly three-quarters of the earth's surface is covered by water. We've learned how to use modern technology to map **across** large bodies of water. Until recently no one was interested to know what was **underneath**, on the ocean floor.

Early depth measuring, such as using knots tied in rope at specific intervals, prevented ships from hitting coastal rocks or bottom. Further out, lowering a lead weight by very long ropes or wires was slow and difficult. But this still told depth only. People had no idea of what was on the ocean floor. They thought mud or sand stretched in a vast, level plain.

The first real need to know what the ocean floor was like came when plans for laying the Atlantic telegraphic cable were made in the 1850s. Then people realized it wasn't a simple matter of laying the cable on the flat ocean bottom because the landscape underwater turned out to have as much variety as the land above sea level. There were valleys and hills, even mountains, as well as flat plains.

Today, we are very interested in the underwater terrain. As food and mineral resources on land become more limited, we are looking more and more to the oceans for new sources of food, oil, gas, and minerals. And there is still humanity's basic curiosity. What does it look like down there? You can't just go down and look. The weight of so much water creates a crushing pressure. It's also pitch dark and very cold down there.

Investigating the depths has to be done, once again, mostly by remote sensing. Today we use echo-sounding instruments, especially **sonar**, a kind of radar that bounces sound waves back from objects such as rocks, undersea hills, and sunken wrecks. Echo-sounders work continuously as a ship moves, giving the variations in depths of the underwater landscape, showing them on a screen. Sonar records lines of information in lengths, not areas. Therefore, repeated journeys across the ocean are necessary eventually to create a linear pattern of the underwater scenery.

Survey ships using sonar can determine the position of any specific underwater point. Satellites help locate the positions of ships even more accurately than ships can, pinpointing underwater locations for adding to a map.

Maps of the ocean floor are based on sonar lines and pinpointed spots, supplemented by measurements of **seismic**—earthquake and volcanic—patterns, gravity, magnetism, and heat.

Underwater mapping is still an awesome task—there is so much water. Two marine cartographers, Bruce Heezen and Marie Tharp, worked out a particular mapping method in the 1950s, showing that probably the best way to draw the ocean floor is as if all the water were drained away, as in a landscape. On a chart, Tharp and Heezen plotted the lines produced by sonar tracking ships, starting from the known shoreline into the unknown ocean, or back to shore from known points out at sea. The cartographers made a **profile** or silhouette of the data, showing the peaks, valleys, and plains and giving the measurements of heights in fathoms. The profiles were then drawn in a three-dimensional picture along the tracks of the sonar readings. The cartographers filled in the areas between the lines or tracks with the information that seemed the most logical. A slope rising at

MAKING A PHYSIOGRAPHIC DIAGRAM

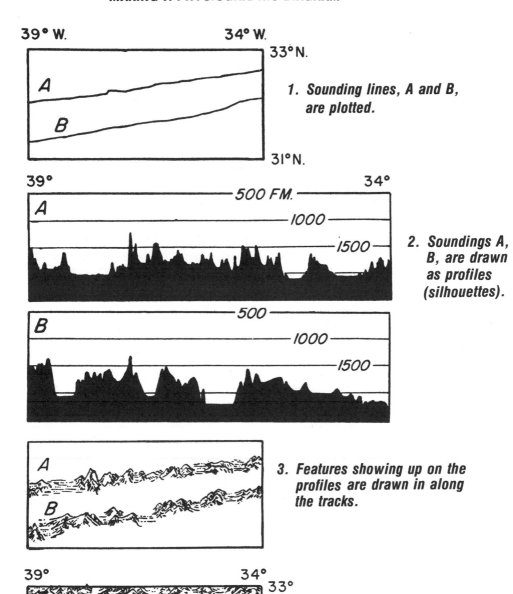

39° W.   34° W.
33°N.

A

B

31°N.

1. Sounding lines, A and B, are plotted.

39°   34°
500 FM.
A
1000
1500

2. Soundings A, B, are drawn as profiles (silhouettes).

B
500
1000
1500

A

B

3. Features showing up on the profiles are drawn in along the tracks.

39°   34°
33°

4. Remaining unsounded areas are filled in using the trends shown by the soundings.

31°

particular intervals could be expected to continue in a similar way based on mathematical probability and supported by geological information. Of course, occasional surprises could occur. An unexpected ridge, for example, might be found by a research ship where mathematicians projected a plain.

The finished **physiographic diagrams** were printed, using a Mercator projection on a scale of 1:5,000,000, during the 1950s through the '70s. The first to be completed covered the North Atlantic Ocean, followed by the other oceans. The latest map, produced in 1977, is in the form of a painting, **The World Ocean Floor Panorama.**

The underwater scene is dramatic. The highest mountains in the world are underwater. **Seamounts** are at least 3,000 feet high, and some of the mountains are higher than Mount Everest, the highest mountain on land. An enormous range of mountains goes through the middle of all earth's oceans, circling the globe. It is called the Mid-Oceanic Ridge. Along the crest of the ridge there is a long central rift valley, a gigantic crack. And at the base of the mountains are wide, very flat plains. These are the flattest places in the world.

The deepest place in the oceans is the Marianas Trench in the Pacific, southwest of Guam. It is a rift in the underwater landscape that goes seven **miles** down. The trenches coincide with faults in the earth's surface, and the undersea mountains coincide with earthquake lines. We are learning more about how and where earthquakes occur, and this knowledge, too, is being put on special maps.

Over the past decades, we've begun to rely less on remote sensing, because we are increasingly able to go down into the depths of the oceans and see for ourselves. We use submersible research tanks—**bathyscaphes** and **bathyspheres**. In Greek, "bathys" means deep.

As part of the French-American Mid-Ocean Undersea Study—FAMOUS—project in the early 1970s, submersibles such as the **Alvin** went into

Part of the North Atlantic Ocean. What it looks like without the water.

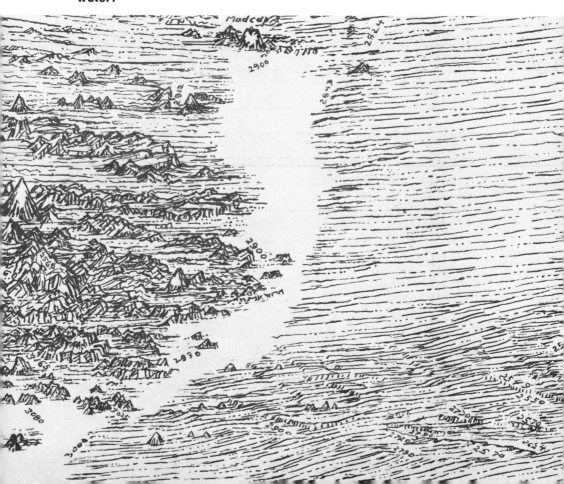

the Mid-Atlantic Ridge running through the North Atlantic Ocean. The crews photographed and mapped an area the size of the Grand Canyon. Submersibles have even been to the bottom of the Marianas Trench in the Pacific Ocean.

We are developing camera systems which can better penetrate the blackness of the ocean depths. In the 1970s, ocean-floor cameras were able to cover small areas. Then a new photography system was invented called LIBEC, for LIght BEhind Camera. LIBEC uses high-intensity flash lamps several feet above the camera, lighting up a much wider area than was previously possible. Thousands of photographs have been taken and made into photomosaics and then into maps of great detail and accuracy.

Dr. Robert Ballard of the Oceanographic Institution at Woods Hole, Massachusetts, is now planning to make a map of the entire 40,000-mile Mid-Oceanic Ridge. It is a vast task. He and his team have spent a third of each year for the past ten years examining the range at first hand. They estimate they have still only seen one-tenth of one percent of the whole area.

For the proposed task, they intend to use unmanned submersibles with sonar and very sensitive TV cameras that will be able to show large areas of the ocean floor. The support ship on the surface will send the images via satellite to mapping centers.

A whole new world is slowly emerging and getting on the map.

Closeup of underwater mountains.

11 WORLDS OUT THERE

We have finally explored most of our earth, even though we haven't finished mapping it. Human curiosity and technological achievement together are now sending us to explore other worlds.

Ultraviolet, infrared, and visible light—these are the raw materials of space cartography. The way we map the planets and their moons is not the chain-and-theodolite, step-by-step surveying methods of earthly terrain, or even ordinary remote sensing. Mapping at such incredible distances means a leap of the imagination for even the most hardboiled scientific cartographer.

We set "maps" of space in the familiar frameworks of projections and networks of coordinates, and give them "equators," "poles," and a "Greenwich"—a prime meridian. Making other worlds familiar in these ways helps us to understand them.

We have already been to our nearest neighbor, the moon. And we had maps of it before we ever went there. We wanted to be sure that when the astronauts arrived on the moon they would know exactly where they were and what to expect.

The moon's appearance was studied in advance and in detail by telescope, cameras, and instruments carried by unmanned and manned spacecraft—Soviet Lunas and Soyuz and American Rangers and Surveyors. Spacecraft in flybys took photographs that included pictures of the far side of the moon, never before seen.

These trips were followed by spacecraft that took TV pictures as they approached the moon. These pictures were received on earth while the vehicle went on to make an intentional crash landing on the moon. Then we learned how to get a spacecraft to make a soft landing, keeping the instruments intact to function on the surface.

Stable orbits around the moon were established so that systematic photography could be carried out. Rockets became more powerful; maneuvering became more precise. The pictures that came back from all these information-gathering expeditions improved as time passed.

A relatively detailed picture of the lunar surface was thus known. However, the main purpose was to choose the areas best suited for a human landing. Rangers and, later, Lunar Orbiters took numerous closeups of the surface for mapping possible landing sites.

The moon had long since been given coordinates, an equator, and a prime meridian. In the nineteenth century, a specific crater had been picked to represent a lunar "Greenwich." "Sea level" was decided on so that relative heights and depths of craters, hills, valleys, and plains could be determined. Using an adapted Mercator projection, topographical and geological maps of the moon were drawn, and a landing site was chosen and mapped in minute detail. The Apollo landing on the moon in 1969 was 100 percent successful with the help of those precise maps.

Later, unmanned Apollo missions carried cameras and other equipment for learning more on-the-spot details of the moon. We began to find out more about the moon's history, geology and chemical makeup. The resulting maps look familiar because they are made using methods that have

Apollo *full shot of the moon*

been used in mapping the earth. But the maps also look unfamiliar because they are, after all, moon maps.

Mars, the mysterious red planet, with its seeming canals and possibilities of life, has always intrigued us. Since the early '60s, Mariner and Viking spacecraft have been looking at Mars. They found no known forms of life on the planet, but it isn't dead either. In fact, Mars is still evolving. It has a giant, perhaps active, volcano, which is three times the height of Mount Everest. Other high mountains, pockmarked with craters, are set in a desert landscape of dust and reddish boulders. Iron in the rocks has turned to rust and gives the reddish color. Most of the mountains are in the southern half of the planet. There is polar ice, and water once shaped the surface of the planet. Wind drives the surface dust into hills and settles it in craters. How do we know this? Mariner sent back images of the whole of Mars. Space probes in flybys and space vehicles landing on the surface took the photographs. Computer-controlled cameras and equipment designed for acquiring geological and other scientific information sent data by radio back to earth. This information was converted to material cartographers could use, together with the coordinates and projections for the framework that every map requires.

We are gradually putting Mars on the map. American Mariners, the Pioneer Venus, and Soviet Veneras have been to Venus, too. It is even harder to take pictures of Venus than of dusty Mars. Venus

Mariner 10 *ultraviolet TV picture of Venus from 440,000 miles*

has a dense cloud cover, searing temperatures, and crushing atmospheric pressure. Space probes burn up very soon after arriving. But several Veneras have managed to get visible-light photos back to earth, and we also have radar images from the orbiting Pioneer Venus. In 1982, two Veneras landed on Venus and took some excellent TV pictures before they burned up. The cameras, set to photograph in opposite directions, covered the whole area from horizon to horizon in concentrated detail. They showed a few mountains standing out above the surrounding plain and deep valleys.

The mapping of Jupiter is now underway. In 1973, Pioneer 10 was able to photograph Jupiter by passing through the asteroid belt between Mars and Jupiter, becoming the first manmade object to escape from our inner solar system.

Jupiter and the other outer planets—those beyond the asteroid belt—are not solid like the inner planets. Their cores may be solid, but they have thick, gaseous atmospheres. Mapping by the remote sensing techniques we have available today is not possible. We can only get pictures of Jupiter's equatorial region and other general areas.

What we **are** able to map are the solid moons of Jupiter. Voyagers 1 and 2 flew by Jupiter's four satellites and sent back images in ultraviolet, infrared, and visible-light photographs showing the terrains of the four moons. Each is very different from the others, and from gaseous Jupiter. It is unlikely that people will ever stand on the surface of these moons because the radiation is so intense that even the space probes "die."

Powerful instruments aboard spacecraft planned for the near future will be able to acquire more information. We will be able to finish our first tour of our universe—gaining knowledge about **all** the planets and moons in it. The more detailed the information that comes back, the more detailed our maps will be, and the better we will understand the worlds out there.

12 WORLD INSIDE YOUR HEAD

When much of our world was unexplored and unknown, legend and hearsay, mistaken sightings and bearings by navigators, and ignorant and fearful reports resulted in mapping places that didn't exist. These places were really the products of wishful thinking. People hoped that some place in the world would be a haven of peace and plenty. They looked for the Isles of the Blest, the Gardens of the Hesperides, the Arthurian land of Lyonesse, Shangri-La. They looked for ideal and idyllic lands in a golden haze of myth "beyond the setting sun." These places were thought to be located mainly in the western ocean, the unknown Atlantic.

The idea of the lost continent of Atlantis is the
most powerful and persistent of these myths of an
ideal land and civilization. Speculation put Atlantis

Atlantis?

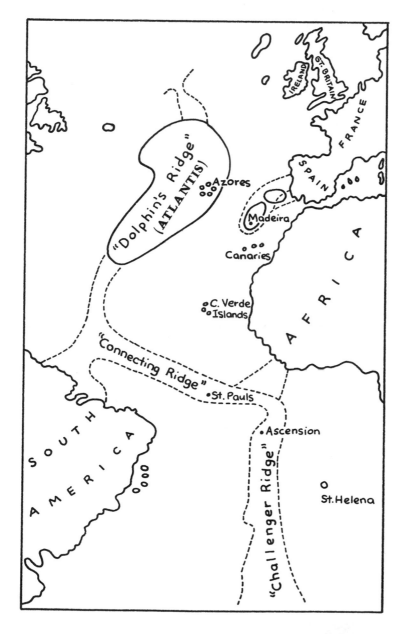

in the Atlantic, sunk without trace somewhere beyond the Canaries and the Azores. Some people thought Atlantis was perhaps America itself.

Other, more ordinary, islands were also placed out there in the Atlantic, just beyond the horizon —Antilia, St. Brendan's Isle, Frisland between Greenland and Iceland, complete with cities and working harbors.

We make maps to try and explain to ourselves places and origins of fantasy and legend—Camelot, the habitat of the Abominable Snowman in the Himalayas, Loch Ness's monster.

It takes only a small mental jump to create imaginary places on purpose. Writers through the centuries have invented their own worlds and have mapped them in detail. These maps can bring a story to life. You need a map to keep oriented in J. R. R. Tolkien's land of Middle Earth in **The Lord of the Rings**, for Tarzan's world somewhere in Africa, and the land of Oz.

Robert Louis Stevenson's **Treasure Island** is one of the most realistic imaginary places of all:

> . . . there fell out the map of an island, with latitude and longitude, soundings, names of hills, bays and inlets . . . two fine land-locked harbors, and a hill in the center part marked 'The Spy-glass' . . . above all, three crosses of red ink—two on the north part of the island, one in the south-west, and beside this last . . . 'Bulk of treasure here.'

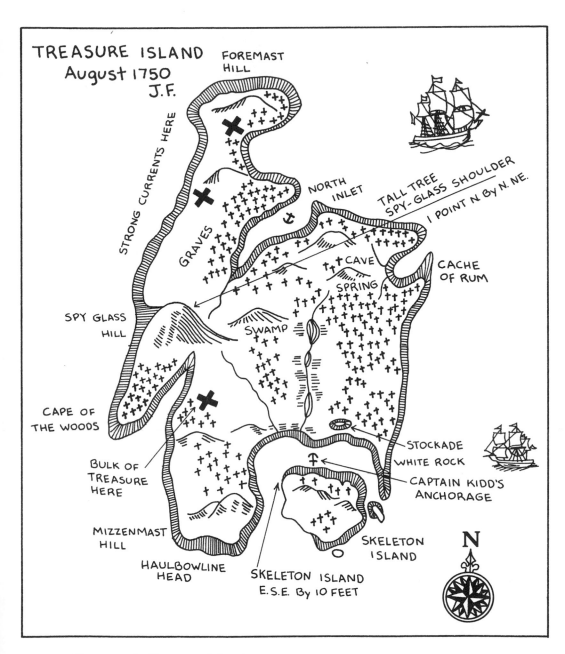

Stevenson's **Treasure Island**

You will notice that the actual latitude and longitude coordinates are not stated, and are also omitted from Jim Hawkins's map. . . .

The maps in Jonathan Swift's **Gulliver's Travels** are both more and less specific than the **Treasure Island** map. Lilliput, the land of miniature people, is shown southwest of the real island of Sumatra in Southeast Asia. Brobdingnag, the land of the giants, seems to be a peninsula off the northwest coast of America. But again, though there is

Lilliput from Gulliver's Travels

Brobdingnag from Gulliver's Travels

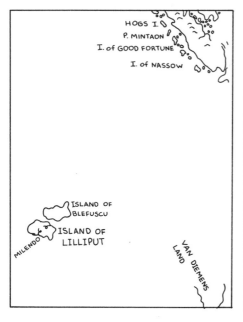

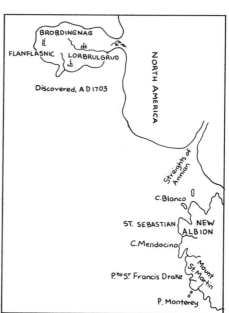

talk of latitude and longitude, compass directions and details of ship navigation, the maps are not specific. Jules Verne was quite specific about Lincoln Island in **The Mysterious Island**, giving its latitude and longitude in the South Pacific Ocean. Maybe he was betting that people would be too absorbed in the story to check it out in an atlas.

James Hilton used the myth of the ideal land, Shangri-La, in his novel **Lost Horizon**, placing Shangri-La somewhere in the remote mountains of Tibet. Mapping India, Tibet, and the Himalayas has been, and is, a particularly arduous task in real life, so it was a safely unreachable place for Hilton to choose. It was unknown, but still in the real world. One could map the area except for the connections to the outside world.

Science-fiction stories are creating new worlds and new "maps" in the universe. And there are the imaginary worlds of movies—**Star Wars**, **Superman**—and the worlds of television from Bugs Bunny country to "Star Trek" and "Fantasy Island." Even video games are full of imaginary worlds.

And some people have even worked out what the real world may look like 50 million years from now.

How about the world inside **your** head? You can make your own fantasy maps. Make your own treasure island, or an imagined city, a new continent, or a space colony. You can use established mapmaking techniques and conventional symbols, or you

Imaginary land

can make up your own and explain them on the map and in the key.

You can start with a real map that doesn't have many features on it—an island or a desert, and add your own ideas. You can make your own measured survey on actual ground into an accurate map and add fantasy names. You can make a sketch map and add monsters—or asteroids. You can enlarge a photograph and add real or imaginary place names.

Use your imagination, plenty of detail, and bright colors.

No map—not even a fantasy one—is ever really finished. The world is changing all the time, and new horizons keep opening up for mapmakers. Do you want to be a part of it?

Books for Now and Later

Brown, Lloyd A. **The Story of Maps**. Boston: Little, Brown and Co., 1949. Reprinted New York: Dover, 1979.

Fleming, June. **Staying Found**. New York: Random House/Vintage Books, 1982.

Girls Scouts of the USA. **Compass and Maps**. New York, 1973. **Hiking in Town or Country**. New York, 1952.

Greenhood, David. **Mapping**. Chicago: University of Chicago Press, 1964.

Kjellstrom, Bjorn. **Be Expert with Map and Compass**. New York: Charles Scribner's Sons, new revised edition, 1967.

Wilford, John N. **The Mapmakers**. New York: Random House/Vintage Books, 1981.

Atlases and Maps

Geographia Map Co.
317 St. Paul's Avenue
Jersey City, NJ

Hagstrom Co. Inc.
450 West 33 Street
New York, NY 10001

Hammond Inc.
12 East 41 Street
New York, NY 10017

Rand McNally & Co.
10 East 53 Street
New York, NY 10022

Underwater maps can be ordered from Marie Tharp, 1 Washington Avenue, South Nyack, NY 10960.

Information

National Cartographic Information Center (NCIC)
507 National Center
Reston, VA 22092

The NCIC can send you all kinds of information on maps from topographical to space imagery. You can also order maps from them.

INDEX

E

Earthquake maps, 80, 82
Echo-sounding, 79–80
Egypt, 49, 51;
  Alexandria, 51, 52
England, 47, 54, 57, 61, 63, 66–67
Engraving, 62, 63
Equal-area map, 40, 51
Equator, 29–30, 36, 50; use in space, 86, 87

F

False color satellite images, 75, 76
FAMOUS project, 83–85
Fantasy maps, 92–99; in literature, 94–95; in entertainment, 97; personal, 97–99. **See also** medieval picture maps

G

Gazetteer, 47
General Land Office (Bureau of Land Management), 78–79
Geodesy, 64
Geography, 50, 51
Geography, (Ptolemy),51, 58, 59
Globe, 27–35, 36, 50, 73

Gores, 39
Greece, 50, 51, 52
Greenwich meridian, 32–35, 70; use in space, 86, 87
Grid/network, 34–35, 36, 37, 75; in atlas, 47; in space, 86, 87

H

Harrison, John, 33
Height. **See** relief; contours
Hiking, maps. **See** topographical maps

I

Infrared wavelengths, 72–73, 86, 91

J

Jupiter, 91–92

K

Key/legend, map, 7–8, 12, 41–42, 46

L

Landmarks, 6, 7–8, 11–13, 17–18, 20–21, 44. **See also** symbols, map
Landsat satellite, 73–76
Latitude, parallels of, 29–32, 34–35, 37,

33, 34, 38, 41, 75; in
space, 86
Political/regional
maps, 42–43
Prime meridian,
32–34, 70; use in
space, 86, 87
Printing, 46, 48,
57–58, 61–63, 69–70
Projection, map,
36–40, 43, 45; in
space, 86, 89
Ptolemy, 51–52, 58, 59

R

Radar, 72, 91
Regional/Political
maps, 42–43
Relief, 41–42, 43, 46,
63, 70, 72;
underwater, 79–85.
See also contours
Remote sensing, 71,
72–76, 79–81, 86–92
Rome, 51

S

Satellite photography.
See photography
Scale, 5, 11, 12, 19, 28,
40, 43, 45, 51; bar
scale, 45;
representative
fraction, 45
Shape of earth. **See**
globe; spheroid

Sketch map, 5–9, 11,
45, 49, 54
Skylab satellite, 76
Sonar, 79–80, 85
Space mapping, 86–92
Speed, John, 63; **Atlas
of Tudor England
and Wales**, 63
Spheroid, 29, 64. **See
also** globe
Submersibles, 83–85
Surveying, 64–69, 71,
73; instruments, 65,
73; underwater,
78–82
Symbols, map, 7–8,
11–12, 43, 46, 70,
71. **See also**
landmarks

T

Topographical maps,
10–12, 18–19, 42,
43, 45; of moon, 87
Triangulation, 65, 73
Tropics, Cancer and
Capricorn, 30,50

U

Ultraviolet
wavelengths, 86, 91
Underwater mapping,
78–85
U.S. Geological Survey,
11, 69

V

W